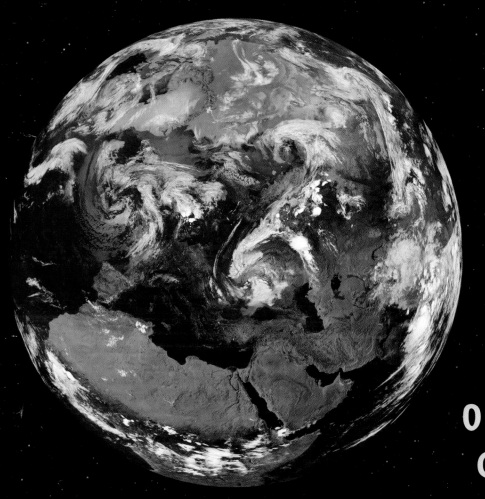

OUR AMAZING CONTINENTS

Continents are the largest pieces of land on Earth. There are seven continents. The largest is Asia. The other continents, from largest to smallest, are Africa, North America, South America, Antarctica, Europe, and Australia. Each continent's landscape has shaped the lives of its animals, plants, and people.

Library of Congress Cataloging-in-Publication Data
Sayre, April Pulley.
Hello, Europe! / April Pulley Sayre.
        p. cm. — (Our Amazing Continents)
Includes index.
Summary: An introduction to the continent of Europe, focusing on its
geography.
  ISBN 0-7613-2151-9 (lib bdg.)
  1. Europe—Juvenile literature. 2. Europe—Description and
travel—Juvenile literature. 3. Europe—Social life and
customs—Juvenile literature. [1. Europe.] I. Title. II. Series.
D1051 .S29 2003
914—dc21
2002011778

Cover photographs courtesy of Photo Researchers, Inc.
(front © Groenendyk) and Peter Arnold, Inc. (back © Roland Seitre/BIOS)

Photographs courtesy of NASA: p. 1; Animals Animals/Earth Scenes: pp. 3
(© Peter Lilja), 5 (middle © Leonard L. T. Rhodes; bottom © Robert Maier),
8 (© Henry Ausloos), 20 (© Robert Maier), 25 (bottom © Peter Lilja); Photo
Researchers, Inc.: pp. 4 (© Dale P. Hansen-Mar Del Photo), 13 (top),
16, 18, 19 (top © Kenneth W. Fink; bottom © Ragnar Larusson), 21 (© Farrell
Grehan), 24 (© Paolo Koch), 26 (© B. & C. Alexander), 29 (top © Dale E.
Boyer), 30 (top © George Haling), 31 (© Andy Levin); Peter Arnold, Inc.: pp. 5
(top © Fritz Polking), 9 (© Klein/Hubert/BIOS), 15 (© Manfred Danegger), 22 (©
Fred Bruemmer), 22-23 (© Fred Bruemmer), 25 (top © Fritz Polking), 27
(© Klein/Hubert/BIOS), 30 (bottom © Jeff Greenberg); Photri, Inc.: p. 6; Corbis:
pp. 10 (© Ted Spiegel), 12 (© Bob Krist), 13 (bottom © Stephanie Colasanti),
16-17 (© Adam Woolfitt), 29 (bottom © Adam Woolfitt); Tom Stack &
Associates, Inc.: p. 25 (middle © Erwin & Peggy Bauer); Woodfin Camp &
Associates: p. 28 (© Robert Frerck). Map on p. 32 by Joe LeMonnier.

Published by The Millbrook Press, Inc.
2 Old New Milford Road
Brookfield, Connecticut 06804
www.millbrookpress.com

5 4 3 2 1

Sunrise on a river in Sweden

HELLO, EUROPE!

APRIL PULLEY SAYRE

THE MILLBROOK PRESS BROOKFIELD, CONNECTICUT

The Grand Canal in Venice, Italy

Say hello to Europe!

It's a land of cities and castles, vultures and vineyards, rivers and reindeer, storks and sheep.

No part of Europe is very far from an ocean, lake, or river. Europe is a watery continent.

White storks nest on the rooftops of Spain.

English sheep

Griffon vultures

The continents of Europe and Asia are connected.

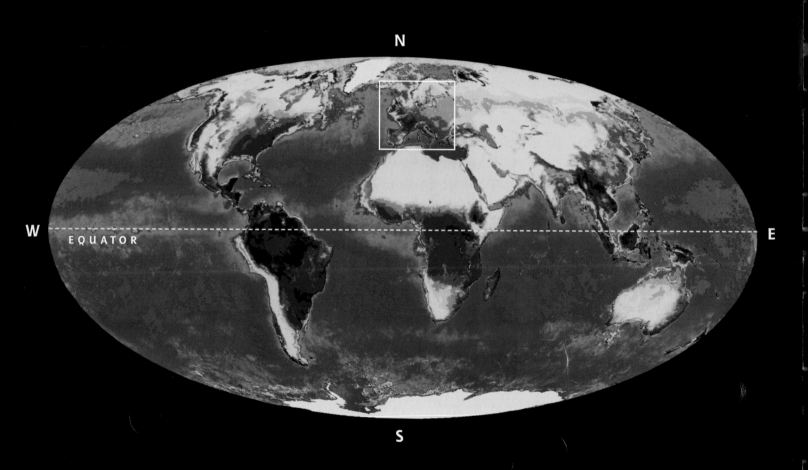

Europe and Asia share one piece of land. Some geographers call this large piece of land Eurasia.

They consider Eurasia to be one continent. Others say European and Asian history and culture are so different that Europe and Asia should be considered separate continents. These geographers divide the landmass at the Ural Mountain range at the edge of Russia.

Below the Ural Mountains is the Caspian Sea, which Europe and Asia share. A real sea is connected to an ocean, but the Caspian is not, so it is more properly called a lake. It is the largest saltwater lake in the world.

The ocean affects Europe's weather and climate.

The Mediterranean Sea along the coast of France

If you trace the outline of Europe on a map with your finger, you'll see it's wavy, with lots of ins and outs.

Ocean water is close to almost every part of Europe.

This ocean water influences Europe's weather. A powerful ocean current, the Gulf stream, brings warm water from near the equator close to Europe's shores. Warm air above this warm water flows over Europe. Partly because of this current, much of Europe has mild winters and cool summers.

A small harbor for fishermen in Greece, on the Mediterranean

A recreated Viking longship

The ocean has shaped Europe's history.

Many of the world's famous seafaring explorers, sailors, and merchants have come from Europe. The Vikings were from Norway and Sweden. Europe was home to the Italian explorer Christopher Columbus and to the Dutch traders who built New York City.

The White Cliffs

Europe has many beautiful coasts.

England is famous for the White Cliffs of Dover, which are made of chalk. Norway has fjords — valleys carved by glaciers and filled by the North Sea. Southern France has rocky coasts and sandy beaches. Spain's Coto Donana, a coastal park, is full of marshes where shorebirds gather as they migrate south to Africa.

A Norwegian fjord

The Netherlands has extended its coastline. To create more land where people can live and farm, they have pumped seawater out of wet coastal marshes. Canals, dikes, and constant pumping keep the seawater from rushing back onto the land.

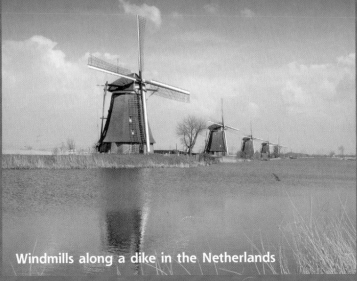

Windmills along a dike in the Netherlands

Europe has large islands.

Great Britain, Ireland, and Iceland are European countries that are islands. Great Britain and Ireland are connected to Europe by an underwater rock shelf. Iceland is not connected to Europe's mainland, but it is still considered part of Europe.

The red squirrel is common almost everywhere in Europe, except in Great Britain, where it is endangered.

Europe has many beautiful rivers.

Rivers are a big part of European life. Europeans fish in rivers. They use river water for their crops. Factories use river water to clean products during processing. Europe's rivers are watery highways that help carry people and products from place to place. Europe's longest river is the Volga, which flows across Russia. The second longest is the Danube, which starts in the Black Forest of Germany and empties into the Black Sea. The Rhine and the Dnieper are two other important rivers. Most of the major cities in Europe were built on rivers to make travel and trade easier.

Sturgeon

Esztergom, a 1,000-year-old city in Hungary, on the Danube river.

French Alps

Europe has hills and mountains.

Europe's highest mountain is Mount Blanc, in France. Mount Blanc is 15,771 feet (4,807 meters) tall. But most of Europe's mountains are not very tall compared to those in Asia.

Europe's mountains are beautiful. They have glaciers, valleys, and lakes.

In summer, wildflowers bloom in mountain meadows. Snow covers the highest peaks. Europe's mountains include the Alps, the Pyrenees, the Caucasus, the Carpathians, and the Urals. Some of Europe's mountains are volcanoes. Italy's Mount Vesuvius and Mount Etna are volcanoes. One of Iceland's volcanoes erupted in 1963 and made a new island, called Surtsey!

Volcanic crater

Eruptions on Surtsey add to the size of the island as lava flows down to the water's edge and hardens.

Hungarian sheep

Europe is a humid continent, with many farms and pastures.

Tulip fields in Holland

The moist air coming off the ocean surrounding the continent makes parts of Europe good for farming. In Holland farmers grow flowers that within hours of being picked are shipped to buyers around the world. Grapes grown in the vineyards of France and Italy are made into wine and champagne.

Europe is the only continent that does not have any large hot deserts.

It does have a stretch of land called a steppe that extends into Asia. A desert receives less than 10 inches of rain a year. A steppe gets between 10 and 20 inches (250-500 millimeters) of rain a year. What rain it gets is enough to grow short grasses for grazing animals.

Social vole

Rare Przewalski horses on steppe

Europe has large expanses of forest.

Part of a taiga forest in Sweden.

A type of forest called taiga grows in Norway, Sweden, Denmark, and Russia.

Taiga has cone-bearing trees such as spruce, fir, larch, and pine. Brown bears, wolves, lynxes, black woodpeckers, and great gray owls live in Europe's taiga. Moose, which Europeans call elk, live in taiga as well.

Central and southern Europe contain deciduous forests. These forests are different from taiga. They have broad-leafed trees such as oak and beech that drop their leaves in winter. These forests are home to squirrels, nuthatches, tawny owls, and willow warblers.

Brown bear

A European Eagle Owl, the largest of Europe's owls

Lynx

Nenet girl leads her reindeer over tundra in Siberia, Russia

Europe has tundra.

A young arctic fox

North of the taiga is tundra — treeless land with low-growing plants. The soil beneath the top layer of tundra is always frozen. Arctic hares and foxes, Norway lemmings, and reindeer inhabit the tundra. Reindeer is the European name for what Americans call caribou.

European civilization began long ago.

The Parthenon, on the highest hill in Athens, Greece, built 2,500 years ago

Notre Dame Cathedral, on a small island in the river Seine, Paris, France

Regensburg, Germany, a Roman town in 179 A.D.

Ancient Greek and Roman civilizations used the oceans to explore and conquer new lands. The Romans especially spread far and wide. When the Roman empire fell apart in about 400 A.D., the Middle Ages began. This is when many of the great castles and cathedrals of Europe were built.

Two sisters from Belgium bicycle to France for the day.

Kids in Estonia take a field trip to an old farm.

Europe has forty-seven countries.

A country is an area of land ruled by a government. Many of the countries in Europe are small. It may take only a few hours in the car or a quick boat ride to get to another country where people speak a different language. So, European schoolchildren often learn several languages in school. If you visit Europe, you might say:

Russian girls visiting Red Square in Moscow

hello, (English); **bonjour**, (French); **buenos dias**, (Spanish); **guten tag**, (German); **laba diena**, (Lithuanian); **buon giorno**, (Italian); **dravstevuyte**, (Russian); **yassas**, (Greek); **dzien'dobry**, (Polish) or hello in some other European language.

Then again, you might just want to start with a smile. That works in any language.

EUROPE

ARCTIC OCEAN

Iceland   Arctic Circle

Fjords

URAL MOUNTAINS

Surtsey

ATLANTIC
OCEAN

Ireland

White Cliffs of Dover
(Great Britain)

Notre Dame (France)

Volga River

Esztergom

Danube River

ALPS

Mt. Blanc

Mount Vesusius

Coto Donana

Mount Etna

BLACK SEA

CASPIAN SEA

The Parthenon (Greece)

MEDITERRANEAN SEA

AFRICA

KEY

- Tundra
- Taiga
- Cool Humid
- Mild
- Warm
- Steppe
- Mountain

0   400 miles

0   600 kilometers

How do you get to know the face of a continent?

Books are one way. This book is about the natural features of a continent. Maps are another way. You can discover the heights of mountains and the depths of valleys by looking at a topographical map. A political map will show you the outlines of countries and locations of cities and towns.

Globes are a third way to learn about the land you live on. Because globes are Earth-shaped, they show more accurately how big the continents are, and where they are. Maps show an Earth that is squashed flat, so the positions and sizes of continents are slightly distorted. A globe can help you imagine what an astronaut sees when looking at our planet from space. Perhaps one day you'll fly into space and see it for yourself! Then you can gaze down at the brown faces of continents, and the blue of the oceans, and the white clouds floating around Earth.